THE
DUFFER'S
GUIDE TO
DARTS

Gren.

COLUMBUS BOOKS
LONDON

Copyright © 1988 Gren of the *South Wales Echo*

First published in Great Britain in 1988 by
Columbus Books Limited
19-23 Ludgate Hill, London EC4M 7PD

Typeset by Facet Film Composing Limited,
Leigh-on-Sea, Essex

Printed and bound in Great Britain by
Redwood Burn Limited, Trowbridge, Wilts.

ISBN 0 86287 943 4

CONTENTS

Introduction

Everyone at one time or another has played darts. A game that knows no class boundaries, it has been played for centuries by kings and peasants alike (well, not quite alike).

Which of us as schoolchildren did not thrill to the story of Sir Francis Drake finishing a quick game of 501-up before sorting out the Spanish Armada?

However, there may be those of you who still think of darts as something to do while the barmaid finishes filing her nails or indeed as a game invented in recent years by Jim Bowen. If you, dear reader, fall into that category, then this book is for you. Please read on, or, as we in the darts world say, 'Thank yew, game on. Thank yew!'

The Dartboard

We really can't start our Duffer's Guide anywhere else other than to point out that to get the maximum enjoyment out of the game you should ideally have a dartboard.

There's nothing more likely to disturb the domestic harmony than for the wife to return from her kung fu class to find that you have, for the past few hours, been practising your game on her overturned coffee-table, on which you have chalked a dartboard (or, worse still, the propped-up lid of the grand piano).

No, even if it means scrimping and saving it is always worth playing with a real shop-bought dartboard. Better still, go to the pub and use theirs.

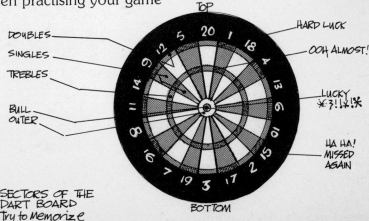

TOP

DOUBLES

SINGLES

TREBLES

BULL
OUTER

HARD LUCK

OOH ALMOST!

LUCKY
·?!!!*

HA HA!
MISSED
AGAIN

BOTTOM

SECTORS OF THE
DART BOARD
Try to Memorize

The Dart

These are sold in sets of three and nowadays the state-of-the-art dart comes in a variety of materials, weights and styles. The flights (the pretty bit on the blunt end) can be interchanged, too. In the early days flights were made of feathers. Now, technology has taken over and some are made from materials developed for space research. The thinking behind this is that if the Americans on a spinning planet can accurately hit a bit of moving moon, you'll stand a better chance of hitting double-top now and again.

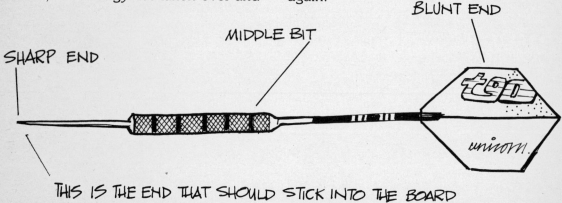

SHARP END

MIDDLE BIT

BLUNT END

t90

unicorn

THIS IS THE END THAT SHOULD STICK INTO THE BOARD

Playing Positions

Assuming you want to play the game with some degree of seriousness and are not content to play in a darkened space beneath the stairs, you should be aware that certain rules have been laid down regarding the distance between thrower and board.

Most duffers are surprised to learn this. Many have in fact found themselves making mistakes, as shown on the following pages. Each of these mistakes has its own technical term.

The illustrations will, we hope, show duffers of the dartboard exactly where they have been going wrong.

1. Too near

2. Too far away

3. Board too high

4. Board too low

9

5. Board should always hang vertically

6. Marquess of Queensberry rules for the correct location of throwing area

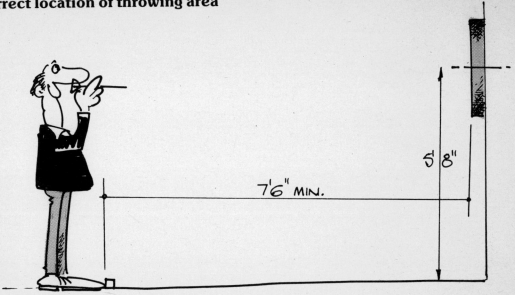

7'6" MIN.

5' 8"

THESE DIMENSIONS APPLY TO MARQUESS OF QUEENSBERRY RULES ONLY

Throwing Stance

The playing stance varies from player to player, but our extensive research shows that there are only six basic styles, from which slight modifications may be made by the individual to suit the player's skill or shortcomings.

You, the duffer, may wish to select one of the following styles and hone it to your particular requirements.

1. The praying mantis

The thrower takes so long composing himself for this that he often goes to sleep before relieving himself of the dart.

2. The telepathic

The thrower in this style approaches the oche quietly and does not release his dart until he feels he has managed to achieve mental communication with the board.

3. The laid-back

This type is happy to throw from anywhere in the room. It doesn't matter much to him if he has to throw over or through a group of drinkers who have invaded the darts area. He doesn't mind at all – as long as he doesn't have to leave the bar.

4. The sneaky

This type saunters nonchalantly up to the board, dart hidden behind his back, then whoosh! Three darts are in before the other players have even noticed it's his turn.

5. The twitchy

This is the nervous player. He'll make several attempts to throw before he sums up the confidence actually to release the dart. If he manages to get a dart into the board the twitching will stop, momentarily, until the next arrow has to be released.

6. The aggressive

This type can't wait for the other player to remove his darts from the board before he blasts his arrows into it, hardly pausing between each throw. Sometimes he throws so hard it takes six people to pull each one out.

Correct Dress

As for all serious sports a certain mode of attire is expected of participants. How you look will often be an indication of your playing prowess. For instance, it's no good turning up at the pub looking like the Crafty Cockney if you can't remember the last time you managed to get three consecutive darts into the board.

1. The 'I'll-have-a-quick-game-until-the-pasties-arrive' type

Almost any casual wear will do if you're this type, or at this stage of your playing career.

Try not to look too flash. It looks silly to be dressed up like something out of *Bull's-eye* if you've got to borrow a set of plastic darts from behind the bar.

2. The league player

The dress of the league player can vary greatly. It all depends, of course, on which part of town the team comes from: for instance, the players in the Windsor Great Park Gin-and-Tonic Lounge Firsts don't dress quite the same as the B-team from the Spotwelders and Ship Rivetters Arms.

3. The international player

You really don't have to be too clever to work out that the person inside this shirt can play a bit. His shirt boasts of his ability. It shouts 'England', 'Wales' or 'Scotland' in large letters on the back, and it's worn outside the trousers, billowing out in all directions. Have you ever wondered why international players wear shirts that are much too large for them?

The reason is simple: owing to the fact that only one player is seen at a time, the powers-that-be can cut right back on costs and have only one international shirt made (to fit the largest player) and the whole team shares it.

4. The exhibition player

To give exhibitions the player must be good and is therefore making a few bob, under both his own and a few assumed names (*see* 'Hustling'). So it's not surprising that he turns out in real showbiz style, looking like a cross between Elton John and Joan Collins.

At this stage of his career the darts-player is entitled to wear whatever he likes. After all, he can hit a sequin at 25 yards.

The duffer would be well advised to avoid playing this type for money – or anything else!

Playing Types

Although many thousands play darts, there are
only five types of dart player – all with the same
objectives but with somewhat wider-ranging
approaches.

1. The professional

The pro will invariably have a nickname, such as the Flashy Flicker, Iced Lightning, Laser Arm and so on. The pro often wonders why there are so many divisions on the dartboard as he hardly ever uses anything other than the 20 segment.

2. The hustler

The hustler is always looking out for the duffer who will foolishly agree to play a game or two – which, of course, the duffer wins. In fact, the duffer doesn't lose at all until he agrees, even more foolishly, to play for money.

The duffer is always able, though never before it's too late, to recognize the hustler – he's the one who's just emptied his wallet.

3. The dartoholic

This type will play darts all day and all night. If he can't find an opponent he'll play darts solitaire until someone comes along.

You can always spot the dartoholic in the pub: he's the one covered in chalk dust, with a spare set of darts protruding from his breast-pocket plus an odd one or two behind his ears.

4. The 'I-haven't-played-for-years' type

This chap always borrows darts from behind the bar and is vaguely surprised to find that there are no feathers on the plastic toothpicks he's been handed.

Customers tend to drift to the corner of the bar furthest from the dartboard after witnessing his first throw.

5. The 'Two-port-and-lemons-and-she's-anyone's' type

This type plays darts in the hope of becoming the centre of attraction. Sometimes she actually hits the board, squealing with delight if her dart finds a resting-place anywhere above 2.

29

Darts People

No matter where darts is played, there are always the same people within the club ensuring the team is correctly prepared and supported.

As a duffer you will obviously want to be forewarned of these people, so that you know whom to avoid.

1. The team secretary

This type is invariably a defrocked accountant or a struck-off used-car salesman who once had a drink with Jocky Wilson on a train.

He can be relied upon to organize the matches and will advise every member of the team of the time, date and venue of the next contest (well – every member except one, the reason being that if the team's one short he gets to play himself).

2. The captain

The captain isn't necessarily the best player in the darts team; he just happens to be a good front-man, looks sober even when he's blind drunk, makes speeches at the drop of a hat and likes shaking hands with everyone.

He will cajole his team into greatness (he once read a book on motivation) and he continually checks up on the visiting scorer's figures – a man whose integrity he doubts.

As a duffer, you should never let it be known that you can add up or have the necessary vocabulary to encourage your team-mates. After all, you don't want to end up being the captain, do you?

3. The charity event organizer

The charity event organizer is a kindly man who wonders why showbiz has passed him by. He is always arranging celebrity darts matches in aid of one charity or another. He will fix up everything for the night, including the raffle, the cabaret and the local press photographer, and will MC the whole evening resplendent in his wine-stained white tuxedo.

The crowds flock to his events, because there is always a rumour that a household name in the darts world is going to turn up as a surprise guest. He never does, of course. This doesn't upset our organizer, though, because he's the one who started the rumour.

4. The adder-upper

Ever since TV's *Bull's-eye* made a personality of its adder-upper there have been queues of people eager to offer their services as scorer at even the most humble of darts matches.

It's all very well being a slick adder-upper on telly, standing there posing like a pop star and muttering 'Take your time, Bert' as the studio lights turn your heavily lacquered hair into a twinkling halo. But turning out in a powder-blue tuxedo and gold bracelets at the Ruptured Ferret to score in an ordinary non-league match could be considered a trifle unnecessary.

As a duffer, however, you should always be nice to the adder-upper. It's surprising how dramatically your score can improve if you keep buying him drinks.

5. The groupie

The darts groupie is usually someone who finds that being a darts-team supporter is a heaven-sent excuse for being down the boozer getting sloshed every night.

She is usually a chain-smoker, and she knows all the darts terms, which she screams from the nearest lager-laden table in order to encourage her own team or intimidate the opposition.

Throwing Styles

The grip and throw that the player uses tells us much about him, so it's well worth the duffer studying his opponent's technique.

1. Delusions of grandeur

Watch for the little finger being raised – this often means that the owner of the digit is a member of the gentry out slumming – or sometimes even Prince Andy in disguise, out for a night with the boys.

2. The couldn't-care-less

Be careful with this type: he's probably escaped from a circus where he used to do a knife-throwing act.

3. The 'Crocodile Dundee'

This one is a typical Aussie show-off.

Don't worry about him – sometimes he misses out on treble-20.

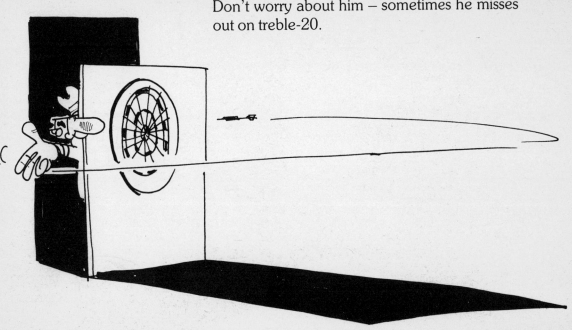

4. The slinger

This type is far more used to hurling rocks or bottles from the soccer terraces.

If the duffer should be confronted with this type of action he would be well advised to avoid making any comments on the subject of football.

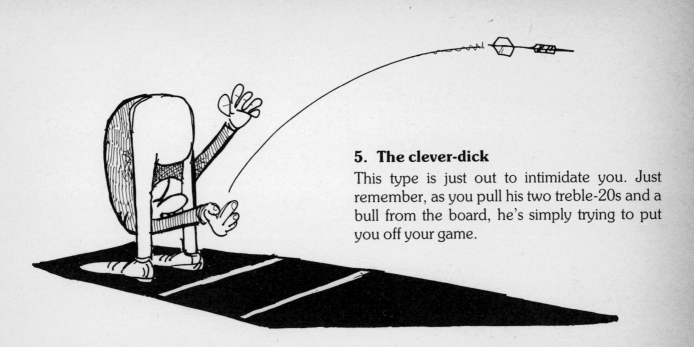

5. The clever-dick

This type is just out to intimidate you. Just remember, as you pull his two treble-20s and a bull from the board, he's simply trying to put you off your game.

Equipment

The duffer will be amazed at the vast range of darts from which he may select. All darts are aerodynamically designed to meet the most sensitive requirements of the thrower and the conditions under which he has to throw.

For instance, you wouldn't use a very light dart if you were an overweight lumberjack throwing in a force nine draught.

The following are some of the more popular darts, one of which should suit the duffer.

1. The Tonto special

Use this dart in extreme emergency or if you are working up a trick-shot routine for the stage.

Advantages: very cheap to make.

Disadvantages: doesn't often hit the board.

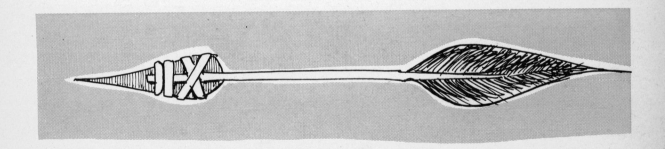

2. The Bowie

This dart has a proven track record. It can split a hair at 50 yards but doesn't do much for treble-20 at 7 foot 6.

Advantages: while playing with this dart you won't get heckled.

Disadvantages: you can't get more than one in a treble-20.

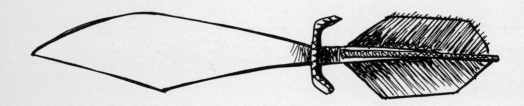

3. The NASA

This dart is packed with the latest space technology and can be thrown with accuracy over great distances.

Advantages: has a heat-seeking tip.

Disadvantages: quite unsuitable for use in the company of smokers.

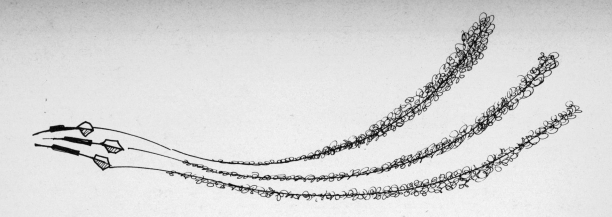

4. The red arrows

It takes a lot of practice before you can hope to master these darts, because unlike other darts they have to be thrown three at a time. Once mastered, however, they produce consistently high scores.

Advantages: they speed up your game.

Disadvantages: the red, white and blue smoke can irritate the eyes.

46

5. The guess-what-I've-found-in-the-attic model

This dart should only be used at family get-togethers when all the players are trying to let Auntie win. It was made when tea-bags were a gleam in the eye of science-fiction writers.

Advantages: it doesn't matter if they become damaged.

Disadvantages: it's difficult to throw them as far as the board.

47

Gifts for the Darts-player

Darts-players delight in receiving gifts associated with the game they love. We therefore assume that you, the duffer, will also welcome such pressies. If you are lucky enough to have a birthday, retirement or parole party in the offing, why not drop a gentle hint that you'd like a darts-oriented present? Maybe one of the following would be acceptable.

1. *1001 Pubs with a Dartboard: a consumer's guide* **(Columbus Books)**

As the name indicates, this is a guide for the serious darts-player to some lovely pubs, scattered throughout the length and breadth of the country, where such individuals can be sure of a warm welcome.

A sequel to this book, entitled *1001 Pubs with a Dartboard where you can also get a decent cheese and pickle roll,* will be published in the spring.

2. The score calculator

This useful little gadget, known as the computerized digital read-out adder-upper, is a must for all serious darts-players whose mental arithmetic is not their strongest point. Simply tap on a picture of a dartboard where you think your darts have landed (or wish they'd landed) and you will be given an immediate read-out of your score and what is required for 'out'.

The Mark II model of this little machine is slightly more advanced and is programmed to scream 'ONE-HUNDRED AND EIGHTY' if you indicate that your three darts have homed in on the treble-20.

3. The traditional dart-sharpener

Of course, if you like that sort of thing, there are sophisticated, hi-tech tip-sharpeners on the market, but the true darts-player is one who appreciates traditional values (otherwise he'd be in the other bar with all those morons playing Space Invaders instead of darts). The Walter Gabriel sharpener is therefore a most acceptable gift.

4. The dart-remover

This makes a wonderful gift, though perhaps never fully appreciated until the recipient's foot becomes impaled on the floor. Then, quick as a flash, the dart-remover can be swung into extraction position (it can be carried over the player's non-throwing shoulder – N.B. Jocky Wilson genuine plastic carrying-strap, only £5 extra) and is actuated to remove the wayward dart quickly and more or less painlessly.

Duffers should always avoid bleeding over the oche. It can ruin one's foothold and adversely affect one's throwing stance.

5. The bandolier

This, too, is a most acceptable gift, housing as it does up to 50 darts which, if you are playing alone, saves all that walking every three throws.

Encouraging Your Opponent to Lose

Duffers should forget all the principles of fair play that they may have imagined may apply to darts. As the poet said, 'All's fair in love, war and darts.'

There are certain tried and tested ploys aimed at helping your opponent lose. On the following pages we offer some of the more successful ways of putting your opponent off his throw.

1. Unnerve him

Almost anything will do to distract your quarry as he's about to throw. Feign a fit, drop a trayful of drinks or pull a cracker. Use your imagination and come up with the ploy that suits you best.

2. Openly admire him

This one, in the vast majority of cases, can be guaranteed to have your opponent hitting anything but the intended target all evening. The ploy is simplicity itself.

When your opponent lines himself up for his very first throw, you place your hand very gently on his bum, give it a squeeze and gaze deeply into his eyes as he gazes in horror back into yours. It will put him off his treble-20 for weeks.

3. The highly contagious disease

This is a well-tried gambit, used to great effect in the career of the legendary W.C. ('Spotty') Hardcastle, who developed it. All you have to do is casually mention that you have turned up to play against the advice of your doctor and that of several people from the London School of Tropical Diseases who all claim that the spots on your face and arms are the symptoms of a highly contagious condition.

If this doesn't immediately put your opponent off, mention 'impotency'. That usually has him handing you the game by default as he disappears into the night.

4. Confide in him

This is a very subtle scheme which can be used only when you play a visiting team.

You, always one for fair play, casually apologize to your opponent for the disgraceful gamesmanship (to which you are very much opposed) employed by your highly unscrupulous club. The board, you whisper, is two inches too high and the oche two inches too far from the board.

He will of course compensate for this and his game will be ruined all evening, for which he'll probably thank you heartily.

5. Dazzle him

This ploy is used by even the most senior of players. If one of the team is wearing dark glasses it's guaranteed that he will try the old 'dazzle' routine.

It's self-explanatory: you try to reflect a light, via your shades, into the eyes of your opponent a split second before the dart leaves his hand.

Although generally successful, the trick has its drawbacks. Due to its complete lack of subtlety it can, and often does, result in the user getting a fat lip.

Psyche Out Your Opponent

Darts is a game often won or lost in the mind before a single dart is thrown. If confidence is destroyed, the game is lost, therefore you should do anything that's legal (or illegal, if you can get away with it) to destroy your opponent's belief that he's good enough to be playing against you. Try some of the following to ruin his mental composure.

1. The big dart

Turn up at a very important match with a huge, dart-shaped case. This will indicate to your opponent that you're not taking the game seriously, therefore you must be very confident. Your opponent will be duly put off by this and, sure enough, he'll be lucky if he gets one near the board.

2. Overdo the move to the left or right

This ploy was used to great effect by the late Flasher McGraw in the *News of the World* finals in 1981. It works like this: as soon as you get your first or second dart in treble-20 you move to the left or right to give yourself a greater chance of getting yet another arrow in that precious space. This change of position is usually only slight; you, however, should move several yards wide of the board. Your great confidence in your accuracy will impress your opponent and he will be in awe of you forever (while his own game is affected in proportion).

3. Collapse

This is another one that works every time and is guaranteed to put your opponent off.

You shake hands before the game, then immediately drop to your knees. With your head back and eyes boggling you start an eerie chanting and wailing. Keep this up for a minute or so and then leap up with a scream. As you come out of your feigned trance, apologize to your opponent (who will assume you've been calling on some supernatural power for help). If your acting is good enough you could find your opponent hangs up his darts and quits the game altogether.

4. Tell him he's not looking well

This is a good one to use when playing someone you know well. Perhaps a club championship match would be the ideal occasion.

As soon as you meet your opponent you say, 'I'm sorry, I didn't know you'd been unwell.' He at once denies being unwell. Surprised, you tell him how poorly he's looking, charitably offering to postpone the game until he's better. He refuses, of course, but the seed of doubt you've sown will put him right off his game.

Congrats, looks like you've won again!

5. The rumour

Hold back for the big moment before you launch this one. Wait, for instance, until he only wants double-20 for out-and-match, then casually ask him if he knows that while he's here playing darts his wife is at home entertaining a young Italian window-cleaner. After this you can be sure he won't get a double-anything all night.

Why Play Darts At All?

Darts attracts a great cross-section of the community. The reasons for the game have little to do with enjoyment of a contest, cultivating skills or wanting to do well at something. The following are some of the surprising answers we received in answer to a recent survey.

I enjoy the boozing.

It gets rid of my frustrations.

67

I hope one day to see a dart rebound off the wire and pin my wife's tongue to the floor.

I enjoy the mental arithmetic.

Daddy was a full-blooded Red Indian.

I'll do anything to get away from the wife.

Darts Terms

There are some terms, frequently used in darts, which the duffer may not at first understand. Here, then, are a few useful definitions.

Oche – A Scotsman's greeting.

Bull's-eye – The pretty bit in the middle of the board which you can only hit when you are trying to get a double-2.

Double-top – What you get when you are aiming for a bull.

Trebles – What the captain orders for the team-members when they've won the cup.

Three in a bed – Rumour about the club steward and a couple of his barmaids.

Out – Score needed before you can get on with the serious business of drinking.

Arrows – Darts thrown by other people.

AAAAAAGHHH! – Exclamation indicating that a dart has penetrated one's person.

Finishing combination – Mostly double-1 in your case.

9-dart finish – Something you've never seen but have heard of.

Darts Injuries

Like many competitive sports and pastimes, darts produces a somewhat specialized type of injury, due to the particular demands on the body that the game inflicts.

The following pages illustrate some of the injuries that the darts-player may expect to receive. Should any of these occur, seek first-class medical attention without delay, or ask the chap behind the bar what he thinks.

1. The perforated earlobe

This is a very common injury. Just look around and see the number of people in the bar with holes in their ears – they have all been standing too near the board while a rank duffer was performing.

Most people who have suffered the pierced earlobe *(Holeinus Earius)* insert jewellery into the hole and have turned the affliction into a many-splendoured body decoration.

2. One-eyed twitch

The one-eyed twitch has been brought on by years of closing one eye when throwing the dart. The remedy is to give up darts and plaster open the offending eye. However, this leads to plaster rash, which looks even worse, so stay with the twitch.

3. Writer's cramp *(Digitus stuckus)*

This is a very painful condition, aggravated by the dart-throwing hand being held in a semi-permanent gripping position. This remedy is simple: change to the other hand for throwing. A real duffer will hardly notice the difference.

4. Boozer's stomach

This is an occupational hazard of the first water. However, if you cannot do without your regular 15 pints a night, make the most of your shape and offer it as an additional table area or advertising space.

This problem will not affect duffers too much because few of them progress beyond the 'half-of-lager-and-basket-of-scampi-fries' stage.

5. The squint

This squint is acquired by the darts fanatic only after many years of peering through heavy tobacco smoke in the hope of discerning the location of the board. For the more advanced cases of thrower's squint a bleeping device can be fitted to the board to give the peering thrower directional assistance.

Bluff Your Way in Darts

It goes almost without saying that you, the duffer, will not want to sound like a rank beginner when you first enter the darts-playing fraternity. So we at Duffer's Guides, at no extra charge, offer some pertinent phrases and sayings which, used judiciously, will make your new-found friends think you know something about the game.

If he stepped down to a 20-gram
it would compensate
for his rhythm.

That's an interesting viewpoint,
but take it from me –
the governing body
won't see it like that.

I'm surprised he
went for the six – he's
stronger to his left.

I remember John Lowe
did that in '86.

I used to use the
titanium-coloured anodized canes
but found them whippy.

He'd be better off if
he moved slightly
to the left.

Quiet, please!
Can't you see there's a
game on?

Go for it, son,
go for it, it's yours!

His throwing style reminds me
of the young Cliff Lazarenko.

If we're going to be strictly
legal, that light is
incorrectly located.

I think I can see where
he's going wrong.

It's all in the stance.
He's far too stiff,
and shouldn't be so erect.

79

In Conclusion…

We hope that the words of advice in this book will have lifted your game from the mediocre to the almost mediocre and that with your new-found skills you will be able to get even greater enjoyment out of this great game – which was, as you probably know, invented by William Tell when he lost his bow and his son left home under suspicious circumstances.

We hope that your game continues to improve and, if it does, we shall bask in reflected glory, content that, in our small way, we have encouraged yet another wayward soul to the path of sheer bliss which is that of a true and steady dart. Game on!